HOW TO TEACH DRAWING

A TEACHER'S MANUAL TO BE USED IN CONNECTION WITH CLASS ROOM PRACTICE; CONTAINING SUGGESTIVE LESSONS IN LANDSCAPE DRAWING, NATURE DRAWING, OBJECT STUDY, FIGURE DRAWING, ANIMAL DRAWING AND DESIGN; TOGETHER WITH A GLOSSARY OF ART TERMS AND A PRACTICAL COLOR THEORY

THE PRANG COMPANY

Published by Left of Brain Books

Copyright © 2021 Left of Brain Books

ISBN 978-1-396-32054-5

First Edition

All rights reserved. No part of this publication may be reproduced, distributed, or transmitted in any form or by any means, including photocopying, recording, or other electronic or mechanical methods, without the prior written permission of the publisher, except in the case of brief quotations embodied in critical reviews and certain other noncommercial uses permitted by copyright law. Left of Brain Books is a division of Left of Brain Onboarding Pty Ltd.

Table of Contents

THE GRAPHIC DRAWING BOOKS	1
DRAWING MATERIALS	3
A GLOSSARY OF ART TERMS	10
A PRACTICAL COLOR THEORY	17
SUGGESTIVE LESSON NO. 1. SUBJECT: LANDSCAPE WASHES *(For Primary Grades)*	24
SUGGESTIVE LESSON NO. 2. SUBJECT: SEEING AS A PREPARATION FOR DRAWING *(For Primary Grades)*	27
SUGGESTIVE LESSON NO. 3. SUBJECT: ILLUSTRATIVE DRAWING *(For Advanced Primary Grades)*	31
SUGGESTIVE LESSON NO. 4. SUBJECT: A GROUP OF OBJECTS *(For Intermediate Grades)*	36
SUGGESTIVE LESSON NO. 5. SUBJECT: DECORATIVE AND CONSTRUCTIVE DESIGN *(For Intermediate Grades)*	45
SUGGESTIVE LESSON NO. 6. SUBJECT: ANIMAL DRAWING *(For Intermediate Grades)*	51
SUGGESTIVE LESSON NO. 7. SUBJECT: FIGURE DRAWING *(For Grammar Grades)*	56
SUGGESTIVE LIST OF ART BOOKS AND ART MATERIALS	64

THE GRAPHIC DRAWING BOOKS

Plan and Purpose

The "Graphic Drawing Books" present, in attractive form, a Course of Study in Drawing, Design and Industrial Work. While these books are based on the same philosophy that for years has been the educational foundation of the Prang Courses in Drawing, the work presented is noticeably affected by the new interests that have recently been occupying the attention of the educational world—the industrial interests and their relation to manual training and the crafts. It is felt that the more our schools undertake to train along industrial lines, the more essential becomes art instruction that is thoroughly sound in its theory and in its application.

The authors of these books believe that the teaching of Art in public schools is upon a sound basis only when it rests upon an understanding of principles; they also believe that appreciation of the beautiful is best accomplished through the study of principles and thorough practice in the elementary modes of expression. These modes of expression should include, not only exercises in nature drawing, picture making, etc., but should also include practice in the useful arts—those arts which are vitally connected with the homes, the occupations, and the natural interests of the people.

The exercises through which these principles are presented have been carefully prepared, in order that they may suit the different grades of children in school. There are nine books in the series—one for each year in the elementary grades and a book for High School students. The beginnings of all the different lines of work, such as nature drawing, design, construction, etc., are found in the book for the first year in school, and these various lines of work are gradually unfolded in the successive years by means of exercises planned to attract and develop the growing interests of the pupil. Changes in modes of expression and in mediums employed, assist the development of the work, and keep the interest alive.

A unique feature of these books is the presentation of a scientific Color Theory that is so simple and so well graded that it is not only practical from the teacher's standpoint, but easily understood by the average child. It is coming to be seen that Color is at the basis of much of our Art work, and that it must be taught scientifically and not by "guess-work." The series of eight Hand-Painted Color Charts in these books are epoch-making and invaluable.

DRAWING MATERIALS

Drawing Books are planned for the use of pupils in the class room. The illustrations present the material chosen for the lessons (such as plants, objects, landscape, design, etc.) and show the manner of rendering. A unique feature of the "Graphic Drawing Books" is that the processes and technique are presented by steps that are illustrated. As a rule, other series of Drawing Books have presented the finished product, and the manner of arriving at such results has often been a puzzle to the pupil and to the inexperienced teacher. The blank pages in each book are to be used for preserving the exercises done by the pupil, so that at the end of the year he may have a record of the work accomplished.

MEDIUMS

Pencil, black and colored crayons, water colors, manila and tinted papers are the mediums employed in the development of the work. In the first and second grades the black crayon found in the "Crayonex" box or in the "Art Education Box," No. 1 or No. 2, is recommended, instead of a pencil.

USE OF THE PENCIL

The pencil is the generally accepted medium for accurate expression in drawing. Results can be obtained by the use of the pencil that cannot be secured in any other way. A pencil having a soft lead is best suited for general drawing in the class room. (The Prang Sketching Pencil, or the Prang Drawing Pencil, "Soft.") A suitable point may be secured by rubbing the lead on a piece of paper. In making a sketch, try to obtain the desired effect by direct strokes of the pencil, that is, do not work over any part of the drawing several times, as this will produce a flat, lifeless result. Keep the work as simple as possible. Study the specimens of pencil handling in the drawing books and note how the direction of the strokes expresses mass, as well as the quality of the surfaces.

Use of Crayons

Crayons are especially adapted for many kinds of decorative work. They may be used in connection with Prang Colored Drawing and Construction papers in making borders, surface patterns, stencils, illustrations, decorative landscapes, still life and pose drawings. The black crayon is an excellent substitute for charcoal, as it is less expensive and does not require "fixing."

In using the Crayons, care should be exercised in layering once color over another so as to secure a harmonious blending. The best color effects can be obtained from Crayons that do not contain wax, such as the "Art Education Crayons," No. 1 or No. 2.

Use of Water Colors

Water color is the most desirable medium for color work. In working from nature, more satisfactory results can be obtained through the use of Water Color than with pastels, wax crayons, or colored chalks. In using the brush, either with color or with ink, enough color should be taken into the brush to make a bold, free stroke. Washes in large masses should be made with the side of the brush, and line work and outline drawings with the point of the brush. In painting masses or in laying washes, the paper should be held at a slant, so as to allow the excess of color to run to the edge, where it can be removed by means of a dry brush or a blotter.

The brush should not be used for cleaning the box. After each lesson, the brush should be rinsed in water and the water shaken out. *Do not wipe the brush*, but allow it to dry, as this will preserve its shape. No smaller brush than number seven should be used.

Decorative Landscape Compositions. These may be Traced and Filled in with Color Schemes.

Decorative Landscape Compositions. These may be Traced and Filled in with Color Schemes.

The Mixing of Colors

The Prang 3A Box contains red, yellow and blue, and black. The first three are known as the Primary Colors, and from them any desired color can be made.

Red and yellow mixed produce orange.
Yellow and blue produce green.
Red and blue produce violet.
Red, yellow and blue produce the neutral tones.
Black may be used to darken any of the colors.
The combination of two Primary Colors produces a Binary color. Thus orange, green and violet are Binary colors.

All colors in full intensity are called Normal colors; that is, they are not grayed. The addition of a third Primary to a combination of two Primaries has the effect of graying the color. For example, normal yellow and normal blue when mixed in equal quantities produce normal green. The addition of red renders the mixture gray-green. Nature shows very little color in full intensity, or normal.

There are many hues of color which classify under the general name of green. They comprise many variations of yellow-green, blue-green and gray-green. These variations of color are in direct proportion to the quantity of the three primary colors.

As has been stated, yellow and blue when mixed produce green. If much blue and little yellow are combined, a blue-green will result; if much yellow and a little blue are combined, a yellow-green will result. If red is added to either of these resulting hues, they will be grayed, little or much, according to the quantity of red added.

Since the combination of red and yellow produces orange, it is apparent that much red and little yellow will produce a red-orange; much yellow and little red produce yellow-orange. Again, the effect of adding the third Primary Color (in this case blue) is to gray the orange.

The same is also true with red and blue, which when mixed, produce violet. A red-violet is formed if more red than blue is used, and a blue-violet if more blue than red. All the resulting red-violets and blue violets may be grayed by the addition of yellow, the remaining Primary Color.

Before attempting to mix a color, analyze it in some such manner as follows: Suppose we wish to reproduce a color which is a blue-green-gray. Since it is a blue-green, it contains more blue than yellow, and, being gray, it must have a considerable amount of red.

In mixing colors, use from the yellow or red before taking blue, thereby keeping the surface of the colors clean.

USE OF COLORED PAPERS

The use of colored drawing and construction papers has become an important factor in the development of Art Education in the public schools of the country. Papers of a firm texture and of carefully selected colors may be used for various purposes, such as: water-color studies, still life groups—drawn with colored crayons and white chalk—paper construction, industrial work, design, and for mounting. By means of these papers beautiful color combinations can be secured, and a new line of interest awakened with less effort than with material formerly used. The lighter tints can be used for pencil work and outline studies in sepia, while the soft grayed colors are suitable for winter landscapes, still life, and figure drawing. The darker shades furnish an excellent color scheme for boxes, portfolios, and toy furniture. (Prang Colored Drawing and Construction Papers are uniform and of fine quality. A sample book of these papers of "Prang Drawing Papers" will be sent teachers on request.)

SELECTION OF SPECIMENS

Encourage pupils to bring specimens for their nature lessons. Select those that will best show the characteristic of the subject. A large spray is better than a small detached portion. Cut away all unnecessary parts. As long as the natural growth is not violated, this pruning will simplify the study.

ARRANGEMENT OF STUDIES

The preparation of the material for a nature lesson is very important. In drawing or painting from plant forms, fruits, vegetables, and still life, the object should be placed so that each pupil can see it plainly. A satisfactory way to show the specimen is to fill glasses and bottles with wet sand, so that the flower or grass will stand upright. Place these on boards across the front desks of alternate aisles. When the specimens are small, additional studies should be arranged on boards placed across the desks half-way down the aisle.

Backgrounds should be placed behind studies of this kind. Do not ask pupils to draw from a small object placed on the teacher's desk or pinned to the top of the blackboard.

Mounting Work

After sufficient practice in any lesson to secure good work has been given, one or two of the results should be neatly mounted on the blank page of the book, opposite the lesson under consideration. This is best done by trimming the edges of the drawing so that the arrangement on the page is a good one. The appearance of the sketch is much improved if it is first mounted on a piece of harmoniously colored paper, allowing a margin of a quarter of an inch to project on all slides.

A touch of "Stixit" Paste to the four corners of the sketch will secure it to the colored paper, and, similarly, a touch of paste to the four corners of the tinted paper will secure it to the page of the book.

A GLOSSARY OF ART TERMS

A

ACCENTED LINE: A line that is varied in strength, being deepened in some places and lightened in others, in order to express certain qualities of form and texture. Sometimes it is broken, the eye seeing to continue the outline.

ACCENTS: Strong touches of color or of dark value, sparingly placed, to bring out certain qualities of form or texture.

ACTION: The expression in a drawing or painting of an attitude, movement or occupation, as manifested in the human figure or in animals.

B

BACKGROUND: 1. A surface or an arrangement of drapery, against which studies are seen. 2. That part of the picture which represents what is farthest from the observer.

BLOCKING IN: To "block in" a form is to indicate by light lines, its general size, shape and proportion, without any attempt to show a finished drawing.

C

CAST SHADOW: The shadow cast by an object upon the surface on which it rests.

CHARGING THE BRUSH: Filling the brush by dipping it into color, water or ink. "A brush well charged with color" means a brush filled with color, but not dripping.

COLOR SCHEME: A range of colors found in mature, or used in designs or in pictures; as, the color scheme of a nasturtium may be orange, red, yellow-green and green; of a book cover, gray-green, gray-orange and black, etc.

COMPOSITION: A thoughtful arrangement or adaptation of lines, shapes, values or colors, resulting in beauty. Compositions may be pictorial or decorative in character.

CONSTRUCTION PAPER: Any paper heavy enough to retain a shape when folded and light enough to cut and paste easily.

D

DECORATIVE TREATMENT: Treatment that does not seek to express fact or reality, but aims to express arrangements of lines, masses or colors, whether from natural or abstract motives, in accordance with the principles of design.

DESIGN: An idea or thought expressed in an orderly way. A design may be pictorial, decorative, or constructive in character.

DISTANCE: That part of a picture which is near the horizon line.

DOMINANT COLOR: A color that enters into and influences all other colors; for instance, in a landscape where the golden sunlight of early morning seems to bathe every object, yellow is the dominant color; on a rainy day, gray is the dominant color.

DRAMATIC ACTION: Acting a scene, an occupation, or a game, for the purpose of strengthening a pupil's mental image.

E

EFFECTS: Graphic expressions or results which suggest; as, sky effects, cloud effects, stained-glass effects, etc.

F

FINDER: A device used to assist in the making of compositions.

FLAT WASH, FLAT COLOR, ETC.—An even tint of color or gray, showing no variations or modelling.

FOREGROUND: That part of a picture which represents what is nearest to the observer.

FORESHORTEN: To represent a surface or an object so as to convey the impression of its full extent, although but a shorter or narrower extent is actually shown. For example, in a landscape the surface of the earth from foreground to horizon line is represented in a very short space, although the effect may be that of several miles. Again, if an object with a circular top, such as a tumbler or a bushel basket, is seen slightly below the level of the eye, the appearance of the top is foreshortened, it appears not as a circle, but as an ellipse.

G

GRAYED COLOR: A neutralized color; a color that is modified by the addition of its complementary, or of gray; as, red is grayed by the addition of its complementary green, or by neutral gray; violet is grayed by yellow, or by neutral gray, etc.

H

HANDLING: Another name for technique, meaning the manner in which the picture is rendered. For example, we speak of pencil handling water-color handling, charcoal handling etc. Direct handling: A handling that secures the desired result without tracing or passing the brush or pencil a second time over a surface. Loose handling: Using the brush or pencil in an easy, free manner; obtaining results directly, without "working" over an effect; "loose" handling" is opposed to "tight handling."

HIGH LIGHTS: The spots or planes of brightest or whitest light seen upon an object.

L

LEADING LINES: The principal lines of direction in an object; those lines which determine the placing, size and proportions of an object or study. Leading lines are not necessarily outlines.

LINE DRAWING: Representing the form by lines only; the opposite of mass drawing.

LOCAL COLOR: The general or characteristic color of an object. As, the local color of an apple may be red; of a tree, green; of a vase, dark orange, etc.

M

MASS DRAWING: An expression of shape by means of a nearly flat tone of color or neutral gray, omitting details, and suggesting only the most important variations in the surface or form; the opposite of line drawing.

MEDIUM: The tool or material used in expressing an idea; as, water-color, pencil, charcoal, ink, etc.

MODELLING: The variations of a surface which express characteristic form. For instance, we speak of the modelling of the muscles, in drawing the figure; of modelling of a fruit, a vegetable or a leaf; modelling means the opposite of flatness.

MOTIVE: The idea or suggestion upon which a design (usually a decorative design) is based. A motive may be natural, as a flower form, or abstract, as a geometric line or shape.

N

NEUTRAL WASH: A tint of gray obtained from ink or black or black paint; a neutral wash may be any degree of gray between black and white.

O

OCCUPATION WORK: "Busy work" planned for definite educational ends.

P

PALETTE: A surface upon which paints are mixed. The cover of the pupil's paint box is designed to be used as a palette.

PENCIL PAINTING: Expressing the qualities of an object by means of strokes made with the flat side of a long lead, very much as a brush is used.

PICTORIAL TREATMENT: Treatment that seeks to express, in an artistic way, fact or reality; realistic rendering.

POSE: The attitude or position assumed by a figure, in order that a drawing or painting may be made. Animals sometimes "pose" unconsciously.

R

RENDERING: The manner of doing a thing; as, "the picture was rendered in water colors" "the sketch was rendered in charcoal," "the music was beautifully rendered."

S

SKY LINE: The line made by shapes, such as hills, trees, roofs, chimneys, etc., cutting against the sky. A sky line is not necessarily the horizon line.

STILL LIFE: Objects without life, although fruits and flowers are frequently included in the term; so are mounted birds and insects, or other animal forms from which life has gone. In common school usage, still life refers to objects selected for their interest or beauty, or which present interesting problems or study.

SURFACE DECORATION: A shape or a group of related shapes repeated in regular order to cover a surface, as in wall papers, oil-cloth, dress-goods, etc.

STUDIES: An object or a group of objects selected or arranged for study.

T

TECHNIQUE: The peculiar handling of a medium, resulting in the expression of the characteristic quality of an object or a condition,—such as the furry coat of a rabbit, the vibrating quality of the sky, the hardness of a rock, the movement of water, etc.

TREATMENT: Method or manner in which a sketch or design is rendered; as, a decorative treatment of a flower, a realistic treatment of a landscape, etc.

U

UNITS OF DESIGN: A line or shape, or a combination of lines and shapes, repeated to form a border, a surface pattern, or other decoration. A unit of design is sometimes spoken of as a repeat.

V

VALUES: The degrees of light and dark in a study or picture. Values refer both to color and to the different degrees of gray between black and white. Values of gray are often referred to as neutral values.

W

WASH: A distribution, by means of a brush, of water, color, or ink over a surface. As, a water wash dampens the paper; a color wash colors the paper; a neutral wash grays the paper.

WORKING DRAWING: A drawing that shows facts without considering appearances; a drawing that gives all the facts necessary for the construction of the object.

Showing Miniature Reproductions in Black of the Graded Series of Prang Hand-Painted Color Charts
These Charts are from "The Graphic Drawing Books" and are sold singly and in sets

A PRACTICAL COLOR THEORY

In business and commercial life, new fields are constantly opening in which a training of the color sense and some scientific knowledge of color are indispensable. Aside from æsthetic reasons, the practical value of color knowledge is now so thoroughly demonstrated that educators are everywhere looking for ways and means that will enable them to make the study of color a feature of public-school work.

The Prang Color Charts offer a simple, and logical development of a practical Color Theory. The Charts should be present in every school-room where definite color instruction is given, although it must be remembered that a Color Chart is like a piano. It is of little value unless it is used.

Color Charts serve as guides and standards, in developing beautiful color harmonies, and constant reference to the Charts will help to clear and illumine that vague knowledge of color which has prevailed up to the present time. The making of Color Charts may profitably be undertaken by pupils of all grades, providing that the simplest steps are taken first. Directions for mixing and spreading the required colors for each grade will be found on the back of the Color Chart planned for the grade.

Spectrum Colors

If we place a glass prism, in the sun, so that a ray of light, passing through the prism is thrown on a white or black surface, we shall see upon that surface the rainbow series of colors. These colors are known as the colors of the spectrum. Each color at its greatest strength or intensity is called the standard or normal of that color. These standards, together with the intermediate colors seen between them, we try to represent by pigments. In dealing with pigments, we find that three of the six colors seen in the spectrum are the basis for all other colors. These three, Yellow, Red and Blue, we call Primary Colors, because they are in themselves elements and cannot be produced by mixture.

The Primary Colors

These colors, Yellow, Red and Blue are elements, each one totally unrelated to the other two. From their mixtures, with the use of black and white, all other colors may be made.

The Binary Colors

The union of any two Primary Colors produces a new color, called a Binary Color. That is, the union of yellow and red produces the binary orange; the union of yellow and blue produces the binary green; the union of red and blue produces the binary violet. Orange, green and violet, then, are known as Binary Colors.

Hue

Hues are the steps between Primary and Binary Colors. Hues are named from the amount of Primary Color present. For instance, to normal green add yellow, and yellow-green is produced; to normal green add blue, and it becomes blue-green. Yellow-green and blue green, then, are hues of green.

Tone

Tone is that quality by which objects become visible to the eye. It is a general term for any spot of color, gray, black or white, as the musical term "tone" means any musical sound or note.

Normal Colors

The perfect standard type of any pure color is known as normal or standard color.

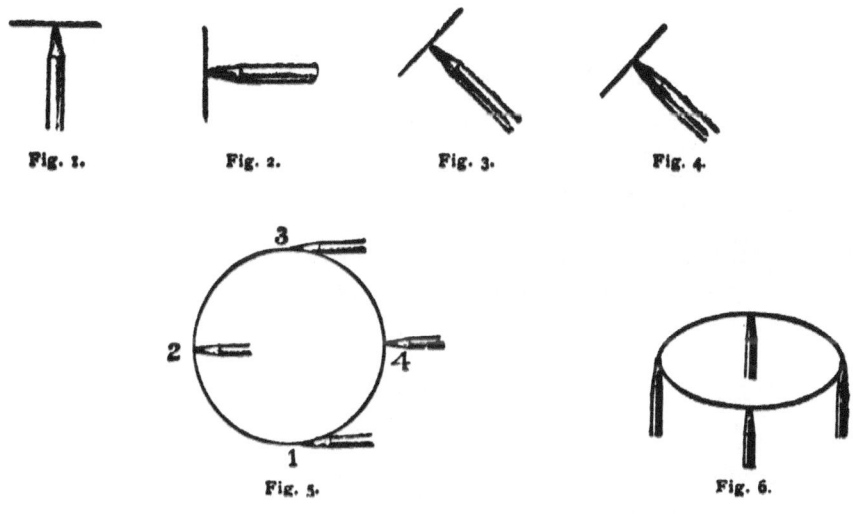

Positions of the Pencil

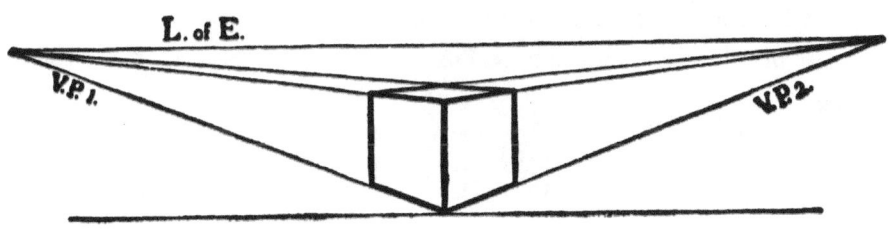

The Cube at Forty-five Degrees

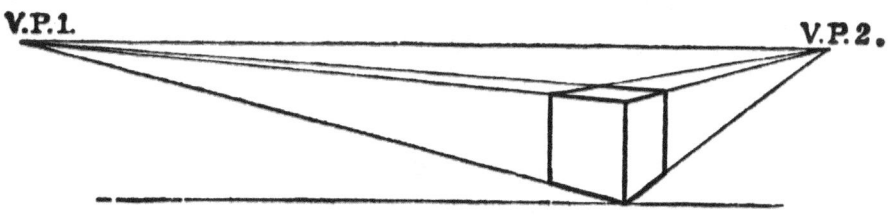

The Cube at Thirty and Sixty Degrees

Value

The quality of a color with reference to light and dark is called value. White has the lightest value, black the darkest value.

Intensity

The quality of a color with reference to its brilliancy is called intensity; for instance, red in its greatest brilliancy is red in full intensity.

Neutral Colors

Tones without a dominant note are known as neutral colors. For instance, neutral gray means a mixture of colors that results in no distinguishing color quality. Neutral gray is not green-gray, nor warm gray, nor cool gray. It is absolute neutrality. Black, the absence of color, is a neutral tone. White, the union of all colors, is a neutral tone. Gold and silver are arbitrary tones used as neutrals.

Tints and Shades of Colors

All tones of a color lighter in value than full intensity are called tints. All tones of a color darker in value than full intensity are called shades. Tints are made by adding white or water to the normal color. Shades are made by adding black to the normal color.

A Color Scheme

A group of colors, harmoniously related to each other and suitable for use in producing a work of art, is called a color scheme.

Monochromatic Color Schemes

A monochromatic color scheme is a group of different tones of one color. These tones may be different values of a color (as orange, light orange, dark orange), or different intensities of a color (as orange full intensity, orange grayed one-half, and orange grayed three fourths).

Complementary Color Schemes

Complementary color schemes show strong color contrasts, and possess the quality A monochromatic color scheme is a group of enriching or emphasizing each other. Complementary colors occur in the Color Circle (See the Prang Color Charts) at opposite ends of diameters. When complementary color schemes are used, the color tones should be reduced by graying, unless a striking or brilliant effect is desired.

Analogous Color Schemes

Analogous means likeness. Analogous colors are those which are adjacent or neighboring in the Color Circle (See the Prang Color Charts). For example, yellow, yellow-orange, and orange form one group of analogous colors; red, red-violet and violet form another. When used in practical problems, analogous colors should be grayed.

How Colors May be Grayed

Any color may be made less bright by adding a touch of its complementary. A little green water-color added to a pool of normal red will make the pool gray red; a touch of red added to a green pool of water-color will make gray-green. Equal parts of green added to equal parts of red will result in neutral gray. It is so with all other pairs of complementary colors.

How to Mix Colors in Half Intensity

Three parts of one color, as yellow, plus one part of another color, as violet, will result in a tone in half intensity of the dominant color, as gray-yellow, one half. Three parts of violet plus one part of yellow will give gray-violet, one-half, etc. Colors in full and half intensities are illustrated in the Prang Color Chart No. VII. Colors in half and quarter intensities are illustrated in the Prang Color Chart No. VIII.

Pigments

Pigments are materials employed in producing paints, dyes, stains, etc. They are not absolutely pure, as they must of necessity contain more or less alloy. Hence color tones produced with pigments can never attain the purity, brilliancy, and luminosity of the colors of the spectrum.

NOTES

The glossary printed in this book provides definitions of technical terms. acquaintance with the meaning of all new terms is an important part of each lesson.

Before the pupils begin to draw, make sure that they have read and understood the text accompanying each lesson. When pupils understand what to do, allow them to do it in their own way.

Have pupils study for themselves the text and illustrations in the drawing books.

Before dismissing the class from the last lesson of the week, teachers should assign and discuss with the class the lesson of the succeeding week.

When introducing a new lesson, do not forget that a recitation, conducted on the same plan as a recitation in any other subject, should precede the drawing.

The best teaching is that which results in fitting the student to study intelligently without a teacher.

SUGGESTIVE LESSON NO. 1.
Subject: Landscape Washes
(For Primary Grades)

Lessons in landscape washes are given to children in primary grades with a twofold purpose in mind: (1) to teach the free handling of the brush and color in blending colors and in spreading washes; (2) to direct the observation of children toward large masses in nature—the sky, the ground, the distance—cultivating appreciation of the beauty of nature under different conditions, and giving children some idea of how these beauties may be expressed. Exercises such as the following give children the joy of color handling, and do not tax them with the drawing of details. Children see masses before they are conscious of details; hence, the representation of sky, earth and distance by means of color washes seems a natural expression of universal surroundings.

Materials needed for each child: Prang water-color box and brush, water pans, 6 x 9 manila paper, trunk-board or back of pencil-tablet, a small sponge or soft cloth, and a "Graphic Drawing Book" for the grade being taught. (These materials may be grouped for each aisle and placed on the front desks; at a given signal they may be quickly passed back, down the aisle.)

"We are all ready for our lesson, but we must not handle our materials until it is time for us to paint. Who can tell me what time of year it is? Yes, it is spring. Wonderful things happen out-of-doors in spring. Who can tell me some of them? (The seeds sprout, the flowers come, the grass becomes green, the leaves come out, etc.) Yes, we all like the spring, and are glad to see the fields and meadows green again. Look out at the sky, this bright, sunshiny day, and tell me what color it is. Yes, it is a bright blue. Is the sky always blue? No, indeed! We know there are many days when the sun does not shine and the sky is dull. Step to the window, Ruth, and tell me if you can see the grass and the sky, too? You can? Tell me the color of the grass. (Green.) And tell me once more the color of the sky. (Blue.)

"Sky so blue,
I see you,
Grass so green,
I see you."

Open your drawing books.[1] Who can find a picture that shows the blue sky and the green grass, and nothing else? Arthur has found it. It is a picture of out-of-doors, and we are going to try to paint a picture, too—a picture that tells of a pleasant day in spring, when the sky is blue, the grass is green, and it is time to look for flowers. Look at the picture again, and tell me whether the larger part is sky or ground. Yes, the larger part of this picture is blue; we see in the picture more sky than ground. Close your books and watch me. I am going to paint a picture for you, something like the one you have just seen in the book. We call a picture of out-of-doors, where we can see land and sky, and sometimes trees, houses and water, also, a *landscape*. So today we are going to paint a spring landscape. Here is a large piece of paper. I wish to moisten it all over, so I dip it into this pail of water. If I press it against the blackboard with a clean blotter it will keep in place while I paint. Now I am ready to moisten my colors. With a brush full of water, I make a stroke across the tops of all the paints. This moistens the dry colors, so that they are ready for use. I wish to take some blue paint in my brush, so I wet my brush again, shake off the extra drops of water, and draw the brush across the top of the blue paint, then carry my brush to the moist paper on the blackboard, and place it at the upper left corner. I carry the stroke straight across the paper to the upper right corner. Lifting my brush, I begin again at the left side, placing my brush a little lower than I did before, and carrying the stroke across as before. Again, and again I go across, until I have filled my paper with the blue wash. If I need more blue in my brush, I dip into the cake of paint again. What have I painted? Yes, a piece of the blue sky. But I wish to paint some ground, with green grass on it. I take a little blue paint in my brush, and then draw my brush once again across the wet cake of yellow. With these two colors I make a stroke across my paper, a little below the middle. What new color have I made? (Green.) Yes, I have a beautiful green, the color of the grass in the springtime. I will carry this

---

[1] These lessons do not refer to specific pages in any book but are intended to be typical and suggestive of the way the teacher can interpret and present any lesson in drawing.

color across my paper, taking more color from my paints as I need it, until I have filled the lower part of my paper with the color of green grass. What have I painted? A little bit of out-of-doors, which we will call a landscape.

> "Sky so blue, I see you.
> Grass so green, I see you.
> I see you and love you, and so I will paint you."

My picture is finished and I shall take it down. Could you paint one like it? Yes, I think you could, if you were very careful to do just as I did. What did I do first? (Wet the paper.) Fred may pass the pail of water and you may dip your papers in it."

(NOTE: The papers may be wet by means of a water-wash applied with the brush. The suggestion of dipping the papers in the water is given to show that there is more than one method in use by teachers of experience.)

Lay the wet paper on the tablet-back, and press a clean blotter over it, to soak up the drops of water. What is the next thing? (Moisten the paints.) Who can remember how I moistened mine? What do we do next? (Take paint for the sky-wash, etc. The class proceeds in this way until all the steps are accomplished, the teacher passing about among the children and guiding them in their work.)

When the children have taken, with reasonable success, the steps indicated above, they are ready for the next step—the placing of distance. The paper is moistened, and the sky-wash added, as before. The distance (*i.e.,* distant trees) is painted before the fore ground of green is added, using a violet mixture, made by taking a very little blue, a little red and a little yellow in the brush, and applying the color in short vertical strokes to represent the shape of the trees. This should be done before the sky-wash is quite dry. The foreground of green should then be added.

In giving these new steps, the idea of distance should be developed by calling the children's attention to the mass formed by trees or brushes that are far away. The teacher should paint before the class, and should then remove her picture, and require the work to be done, step by step, by the children, under her guidance.

SUGGESTIVE LESSON NO. 2.
SUBJECT: SEEING AS A PREPARATION FOR DRAWING
(For Primary Grades)

No expression, either verbal or graphic, can be vital or adequate unless it comes from a vital and adequate impression. In other words, in order to speak well, we must have something to say, and in order to paint or draw well, the first necessity is, also, that we have something to say. In children's drawings, weak and feeble results are due more frequently to lack of knowledge of the subject, or lack of interest in it, than to lack of ability to express. The presentation of a lesson in such a way as to awaken interest, and to call attention to vital points is just as important as technical ability in the use of mediums. The teacher who can teach well is more apt to succeed in this work than the artist who does not know how to present the lessons so as to direct the children's observation to essential points.

The exercise here given is supposed to precede a lesson in painting from a flower, and the specimen selected is a growth of the brown-eyed Susan.

Points to be developed: name of plant; where found; character of growth; color and shape of blossoms; color and shape of leaves; comparison of particular growth with other growths of brown-eyed Susan; adaptation of the size of the drawing paper to the shape and size of the specimen to be drawn.

The teacher is before her class with a fine specimen of the brown-eyed Susan in her hand, and with several other specimens in reserve.

"Who can tell me the name of this flower?" (Several names will probably be given, such as daisy, sunflower, etc. The teacher decides upon or gives the correct name.) Yes, it is called the brown-eyed Susan. I wonder how it came to be called that? (Because the center or 'eye' of the flower is a beautiful brown.) Where does it grow? Do we plant its seeds and raise it in our flower gardens? No, it is a wild flower, and we find it in the fields and meadows, and along country roads. Who can tell the color of the blossom? (The children will probably answer 'yellow.') Yes, some people would call it yellow, but it is not the yellow of the dandelion or buttercup; it is a deeper and richer color, like the outside of a certain fruit that we all like. Who knows what the color is? (Orange.) Yes, the brown-eyed Susan has orange petals, and a deep brown center. What is the shape of the blossom? (Round, like the daisy or sunflower.) There are many flowers that are round like this—that have a central part with petals growing around it. Such flowers are not hard to paint, for we can make each petal with a single stroke of the brush. Who can tell me something about the leaves? They are green, of course, and what shape are they? (Somewhat long and pointed.) Where is the widest part of each leaf? (Near the middle.) Does each leaf grow by itself on the stem? (No, they grow in pairs.) When leaves grow in this way we say they are 'opposite.' Look at the base, or flower part of a leaf and see if there is a little stem. Yes, each leaf has a short stem. Remember that, when you paint or draw this plant. Are all the leaves the same size? (No, those at the top are smaller.) Now look at the main stem of the plant, and tell me where it is the largest. (It is bigger at the lower part.) Yes, the stem is larger and stronger near the ground, and grows smaller at the upper part, near the flower. Do you remember the golden-rod? Can you tell me whether the stem of the brown-eyed Susan is like that? (No, the golden-rod has a leafy stem; there are so many leaves that you can hardly see the stem.) The stem of the brown-eyed Susan is very plainly seen, and stands up quite straight and stiff. Now, let us open our Drawing Books. What do you see? (A picture of the brown-eyed Susan.) Yes, it is a picture of another spray of this same plant. Tell me how it differs from the one we have. (The children tell various points of difference and resemblance.) The picture in the book does not show the beautiful colors, but it tells us so many other things that we know which plant is meant. Look at the two blossoms in the book. We seem to be looking across the tops of the blossoms; they are not turned directly toward us. In this position some of the petals look a little longer than the others. Who can tell where the longest petals are? (At the sides.) Where are the shortest petals? (At the back.) Notice how the leaves are drawn. Are they pressed down? (No, they seem to curve and bend, the way they do in the plant.) Yes, the leaves and flowers look alive in the picture, and are not drawn as though they were pressed flat in a book. We must remember all these things in our lesson tomorrow. When we paint, we are to sketch very lightly with a brush-line of faint color the main stem of the flower we are looking at. We then decide where the dark 'eye' or center of our flower is to be placed, and paint that first. Then with a single brush stroke, we paint each petal, remembering that some of the petals look longer than others. After drawing the stem with a stroke of green, we try to draw the leaves with the side of the brush, making the stroke curve, so that the leaves will not look flat. Study again the leaves in the picture, to see if they were painted in that way.

A Flower Study Well Composed and Correctly Spaced

"Today we have become acquainted with our flower. Tomorrow, I will place plenty of brown-eyed Susan's where you can see them plainly, and your pictures will tell me how well you remember your lesson of today."

NOTE: In plant drawing it is of the utmost importance that specimens placed so that each pupil can see one plainly. Again, the teacher should see that the size and shape of the paper upon which the children place their drawing or painting should correspond to the size and shape of the specimen that they study.

A Growth of Cherries, Decoratively Treated

SUGGESTIVE LESSON NO. 3.
SUBJECT: ILLUSTRATIVE DRAWING
(For Advanced Primary Grades)

In our desire to acquaint little children with the use of materials and with certain processes or methods of work, we are apt to forget that they should have, at frequent intervals, an opportunity to express themselves in a free and unhampered way. Without such exercises we shall fail to develop in the children any individuality of expression or any great freedom; they will fall into the habit of expressing, in the teacher's way, some idea that the teacher has imposed upon them. To offset this tendency, illustrative drawing is most valuable, and should not be neglected. In such work the teacher may help the children to think definitely about what they are to draw, but she is not to tell them what to draw, nor how to draw it. Neither is she to criticize, except incidentally, the technical quality of results; she is to look for the story-telling quality as the most important point, and judge very largely from that as to the excellence of the work.

In presenting for the first time an exercise of this kind, a little device known as a "finder" will be of great assistance. This consists of a piece of cardboard or stiff paper, measuring four by five inches, in which a rectangular opening is cut out; the opening measuring two by three inches. A finder and Drawing Book should be on each child's desk.

"In your Drawing Book are many pictures —pictures of out-of-doors, of flowers and plants, of children, of animals, and of many things that you see about you, or of things that you are sometime going to make. On some pages of your Drawing Book there are pictures that have a line around them, like a little frame. Who can tell me what is in the frame?"

"A picture of out-of-doors in winter,—some bushes, the sky, a girl with a sled, etc."

"On other pages are colored pictures that look almost alike, and yet which are not just alike, after all. Who can tell me what the first picture shows?"

"Just the sky and the ground."

"Yes, it is like our first little painting of the landscape. Is there anything in the second picture that we do not see in the first? Who can tell?"

"There are a few clouds in the second picture."

"What is in the third picture that is not in either of the others? Yes, we can all see plainly some distant trees. It is the best picture of the three to look at, because it tells us of the blue sky, the green fields, and a pleasant grove, or woods, where we can sit in the shade and eat our lunch under the big trees. Turn to another picture in your Drawing Book. Who can tell me about this picture?"

(The children describe what is shown, guided by the teacher's questioning.)

"Now, Alice may find a picture in the book,—the one she likes the best of all,—and Ruth may describe the picture that Alice has chosen. You see that pictures tell us stories, sometimes better than words can tell us. You would not like your Drawing Book or your reader so well if they had no pictures in them, would you? Let us close our books, and find pictures somewhere else. On your desk you will find something that looks like a little picture-frame. We call it a finder, and you will see how useful it is in helping us to find pictures. Take up your little frames; hold them with both hands in front of you, like this." (The teacher holds hers in both hands, at arm's-length, straight out in front, with the opening opposite her eyes.) "What do you see in your picture, Mary?"

"I see the teacher's desk, a chair in front of it, and back of that the blackboard."

"What do you see, Harold?"

"I see the window-sill, with the plants and the gold-fish."

"And what does Henry see?"

"I see Jennie's head and shoulders, the bow on her hair, and the desk in front of her."

The finders may be moved about and new pictures found, the exercise being planned to assist in concentrating the attention on some definite space.

"You have seen today how many pictures may be found inside these little frames. I am going to ask you to take the frames home with you, and look at something on the way, or at home, that you think would make an interesting picture. Tomorrow you may tell me what you saw."

Upon resuming the exercise, the following day, the children are asked to tell what pictures they saw through their finders. The answers may be somewhat as follows:—

"I saw a high fence with a bush sticking out over the top; the top of a house showed in the finder, too."

"I saw a dead tree, with a bird's nest on one limb, and a big white cloud in the sky, behind the tree."

"I saw a man carrying a bag upon his back. A little black dog was trotting after him."

"I saw some boys playing marbles on the sidewalk."

"I saw a store, with some barrels and boxes and all kinds of fruit outside."

The teacher who is able to sketch upon the black board will find the interest (and hence the memory and imagination) much increased if she sketches very quickly upon the blackboard several of these pictures described by the children, first drawing an enclosing line to represent the finder, or the limiting space of the picture. In such work use the side of a short piece of chalk and draw only the important masses.

"Now you may take crayon and paper and tell me what you saw—not in words but in pictures. I will see if I can tell what you have seen. Do not explain in words, but let your pictures tell the story."

The next phase of this work is the illustration of some definite thought, supplied or suggested by the teacher. Up to this point the pupils have been going their own separate ways, each providing the idea or thought to be illustrated. Now, they start with a common thought, to be followed out or expressed as each little mind and imagination may picture it. At first, a topic suggesting some story with which the children are familiar will be best:

"Once upon a time there was an old woman who lived in a little hut on the top of a hill."

"She always wore a black dress, with a white apron tied with a big bow in the back. On her head she wore the queerest sunbonnet you ever saw."

> "Saw the moon rise from the water,
> Rippling, rounding from the water.
> Saw the flecks and shadows on it,
> Whispered, 'What is that, Nokomis?'"

"Jack be nimble, Jack be quick,
Jack, jump over the candlestick."

Keep the quotations short, giving just enough to convey a picture that shall be bold and simple. Colored crayons or water-colors are a great assistance to such work, though it can be done with charcoal, black crayon, or with brush and ink.

Groups in Outline. Well Composed and Correctly Spaced

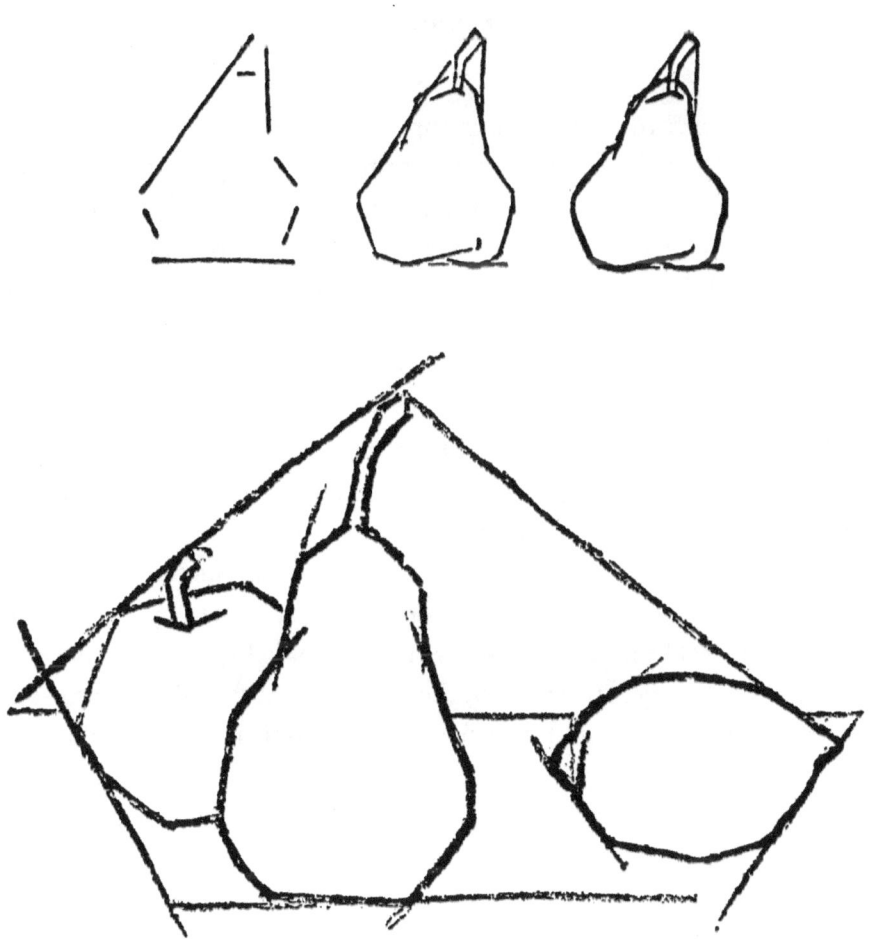

Showing Blocked-in Sketches of a Group of Fruits

SUGGESTIVE LESSON NO. 4.
Subject: A Group of Objects
(For Intermediate Grades)

A successful lesson in object or group drawing depends very largely upon three things: (1) on the selection made of the objects or groups to be drawn; (2) on the number and placing of these objects or groups; (3) on the points developed by an intelligent presentation of the lesson by the teacher.

It is essential that as many groups shall be provided as there are aisles in the room,—a group to be placed on boards across every other aisle on the front desks, and a second group placed half-way down the same aisle. This enables every pupil in the room to get a good view of some group, and permits individual observation, which is the end sought. Never ask all the pupils in a room to draw from an object or a group placed upon the teacher's desk. This is a very common and serious mistake.

The points to be developed in the presentation of such a lesson are as follows: choice of objects of simple construction that seem to belong together; that are not just alike in size; that show contrasts of light and dark values; the arrangement of the group for unity; the expression in the drawing of proper size, relative proportions and distance; the characteristic shape or outline of each object in the group.

Materials: The Drawing Book intended for this grade, pencil and 9″ x 12″ manila paper on each desk.

"We are going to make a study today of a group of two objects, and I want you to observe the group before you so carefully that you will be able to draw, after this, any group of two objects that you may see. Look at the group before you. Helen, what are the objects in your group?"

"A teapot and a cup."

"Fred, what is in your group?"

"A pitcher and a bowl."

"Grace, what have you to draw?"

"I have a saucepan and a turnip."

"What have you, Fred?"

"A glass with a straw in it and a lemon."

"Charles may tell what he has."

"An earthen kettle and a beet."

"What has Ethel?"

"A watering-pot and a flower-jar."

"The groups are all different, you see, yet they are made of common things that we use at home. I have put in them the things that are often used together, and are often seen in each other's company. This we must always be careful to think about when we are arranging objects. Suppose I had arranged a group of this kind: (the teacher arranges the watering-pot and the lemon together); or like this: (the flower-pot and the sauce pan); or like this: (the glass with straws and the turnip), you would see that the groups would seem strange. We would have an effect like discord in music. So, you see that we must look for *harmony* in our groups as well as in our music.

"Look at your groups again, now that I have arranged them as they were before, and tell me about the sizes of the objects. Belle, are your two objects of the same size?"

"No, the teapot is larger than the cup."

"In each group you will find that there is a difference in size; there is something tall and something short, so that the shapes of the objects in your drawing will not be of the same size, or their tops appear on the same level." We must have variety in our drawing.

"Look again at your group, William; you are looking at the pitcher and the bowl. Which is the darker of your two objects?"

"The bowl is dark brown, and the pitcher is light, with a blue band near the top."

"Belle, which is the darker object in your group?"

"The saucepan; the turnip is almost white, and the outside of the saucepan is dark blue."

"You will find that each of your groups has a dark object and a light object. Even in this group (the lemon and the glass) the glass looks very light because it has a light paper behind it as a background, and the lemon is darker, in effect, than the glass. We have spoken before of this quality of light and dark as *value*. So we see that it is well to have in our groups a contrast or variety of values.

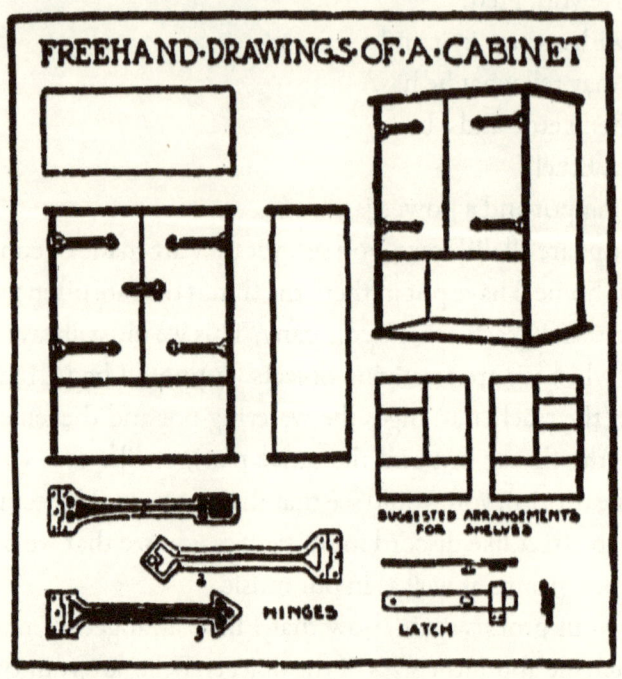

A Working Drawing of Three Views, a Perspective Sketch and Detail Drawings

Composition and Spacing of a Group of Objects

How to Paint and Mount a Maple Leaf

"Once again study the group before you. This time observe carefully how the objects are placed in relation to each other. You do not see them just alike, of course, for some of you are sitting on the left of the group you are to study, and some are on the right. But you can tell me something that is true about the arrangement of the objects.

"Martha, can you tell me how your objects are placed?"

"They are placed near together."

"Yes, they are near together; but are they in a row?"

"No; one object is a little ahead of the other."

"That is right; in all the groups one object is a little ahead of the other, and today I have placed in each group the small object a little in advance of the larger." John, do you see a space between your objects?"

"No. I am looking at the teapot and the cup, and the cup laps over and hides a part of the teapot."

"Charles, you are sitting on the other side of the aisle; how do you see it?"

"I see a little space between the objects! I can see all of the teapot and all of the cup."

"I wish you would all look at your groups, and find out whether your objects are spaced a little, or whether one object hides a part of the other. (The children observe, and make the various reports.) You see it does not matter whether the objects are somewhat spaced or whether one hides a part of the other. If spaced, the distance between them must not be so great that we lose the idea of a group; and if they seem to overlap, one object must not stand directly in front of the other, like this (demonstrates), so that the shape of the group is unpleasant.

"There is one more thing that we must find out before we begin to draw. Look again at your group. Observe the height of the taller and farther object. See where the top of the nearer and shorter object comes in relation to this height. Is it as high as the middle of the farther object, or is it below or above the middle? Nellie, you are looking at the lemon and the glass. Tell me how high on the glass the top of the lemon appears."

"The highest part of the lemon comes below the middle of the glass."

"Do you know, Nellie, where you would draw the lower curve of the lemon in relation to the base of the glass?"

"It would come below the base of the glass."

"That is right. This is a very important point, and we will be able to understand it better if we look at some pictures. Open your Drawing Book to a page of object drawing. Find a picture of a group something like the groups you are studying. There are two objects, a kettle and a beet. Look at the drawing of the beet, and tell me where the highest part of the curve comes in relation to the kettle."

"It comes a little above the bottom, and hides a small part of the surface of the kettle."

"Where is the lowest part of the beet, in relation to the kettle?"

"It is quite a little below the bottom of the kettle."

"Turn to another page of object drawing. Which seem to be nearer to us, the pumpkin or the bushel basket?"

"The pumpkin."

"Yes. Notice that it is drawn *lower on the paper* than the basket. Turn to another page showing object drawing. Which is the nearest thing to us in this picture?"

"The boy."

"Yes, the boy is a very little nearer to us than the tree, and both tree and boy are much nearer than the distant trees. You will find that *the nearest thing to us in pictures is always drawn lowest on the paper*. The only other question we have to settle is how much lower on the paper we must place objects that are near in order to express just the right amount of distance.

"Close your books and place your papers in position to draw. Before you draw the shapes of the objects in your group, I wish you to place four short dashes to show the height and width of the larger and farther object. Then place four dashes to show the height and width of the smaller and nearer object, being sure that you place this second set of four dashes in the right relationship to the first set. When this is done, draw through these dashes light pencil lines that will show the general shapes of the objects. Then I will pass about the room, and see if you have located your objects to express your group truthfully."

The work should be carefully looked after at this stage, as the expressions of distance and of relative proportions are more important at this time than the careful drawing or the finish of the objects. The pupil should not be allowed to "finish" his drawing, even in outline, until he is able to block in the objects to show distance and relative proportions. When he can do this, not only from one group, but from any simple group of two objects, he may draw the outlines carefully, working over the light "blocking-in" lines, and may finish his drawing in accented outline or in values, as the teacher may decide.

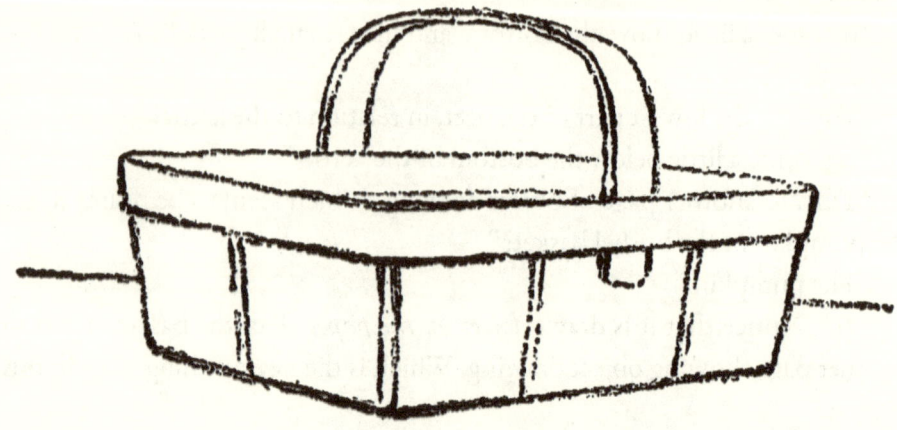

A Perspective Sketch from the Object

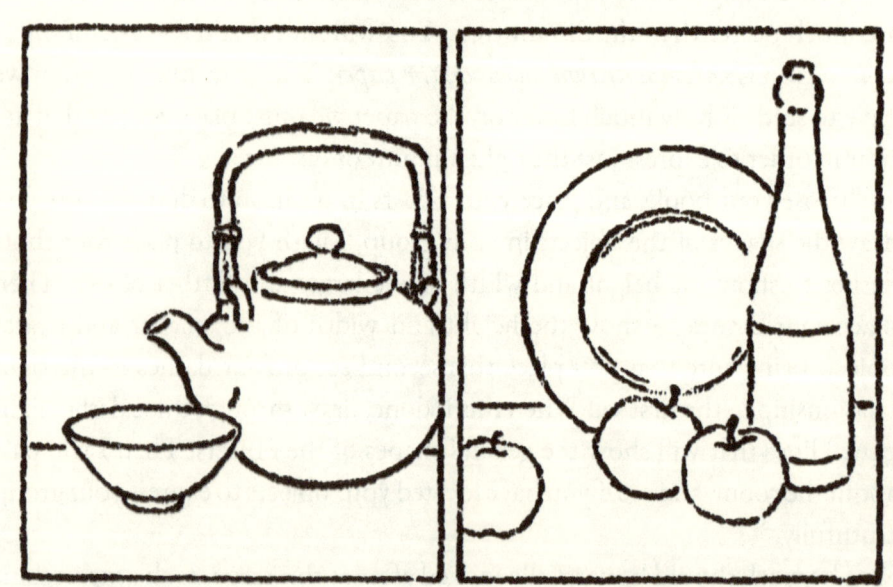

Showing Grouped Objects Treated in Outline
Note the Composition and Spacing

Vase Forms

Mass Drawings from Common Objects

SUGGESTIVE LESSON NO. 5.
Subject: Decorative and Constructive Design
(For Intermediate Grades)

Before taking up the particular lesson outlined below, the pupils are supposed to have accomplished the work usually covered in the Primary Grades. They are ready for this lesson, with circle-maker, test-square, pencil, manila practice paper, scissors, some large simple flower like the dog-wood blossom, and the Drawing Book on each desk.

"We are to have a most interesting lesson today, in which we shall use our circle-makers and test-squares. As a beginning, you may draw a circle on your papers, whose radius is 1½ inches. What diameter will your circle have, Kate?"

"If the radius is 1½ inches, the diameter will be three inches."

"Very well. Let the circumference of your circle be drawn with a light pencil-line, and be sure that the circle measures three inches in diameter. Using your test square at the center of your circle, rule two radii at right angles to each other. Repeat to secure four right angles. Now how many diameters have you in your circle, James?"

"We have two diameters."

"How many radii, Julia?"

"We have four radii."

"These radii divide the circle into how many equal parts, George?"

"Into four equal parts."

"Yes, we have four spaces, just alike in shape and size, in our circular field. Let us suppose that we wish to make a decoration, something like a rosette, within our circle. How many units, or shapes, would the divisions already made within our circle naturally suggest?"

"We could repeat a unit or shape four times, placing one shape in each quarter of our circle."

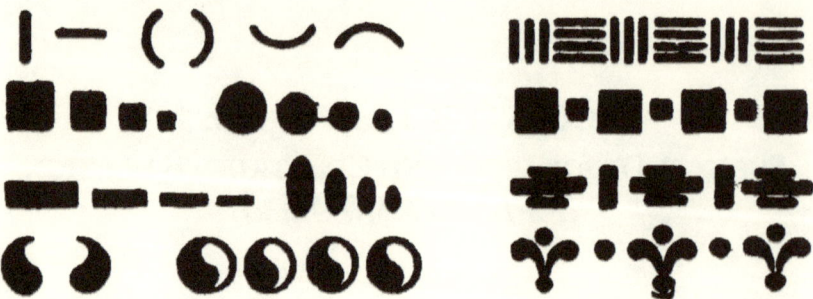

Simple Elements of Design

Two Decorative Arrangements of Nature Forms

Insect and Flower Motifs used in Design

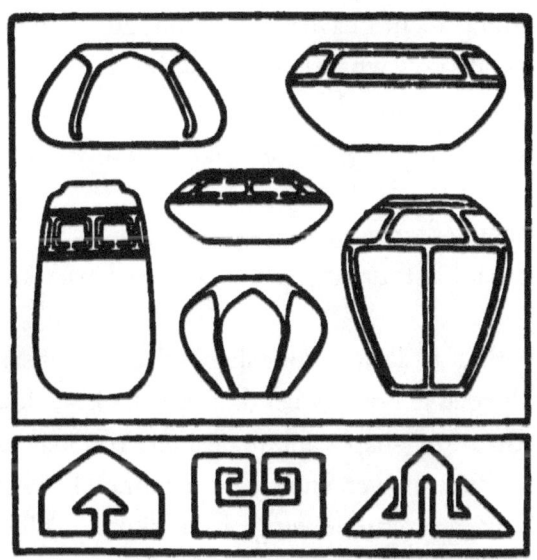

Structural Designs

The Use of Borders

"Yes. There are many arrangements that we might make, but I think you will know what arrangement I have planned for you if you look at the flower on your desk. Do you know what flower it is, Mabel?"

"So it is. Some other simple flower might have been selected, but the dogwood blossom was particularly good for our lesson today. Do you know why, Frank?"

(Frank examines the flower.)

"I think because it has four large petals, and we have four spaces to fill in our circle."

"Yes, it will be easier to arrange four shapes than five or six or seven, in the circle as we have divided it. Some other day we will plan a design in which we will repeat more than four shapes about a center. You may each pull off one of the four petals of your flower, and lay it on your desk, where its shape may be plainly seen. Make a careful drawing of it in life size. What do you notice about its shape, Edward?"

"The part farthest from the center is widest and the petal has a little scallop or notch in the top."

"Yes, that notch or scallop is one of the characteristics of the dog-wood. Kate, will you look at the petal and tell me if the curve is exactly alike on both sides, so that if you folded it in the middle both sides would be precisely alike?"

"No, the two sides are not exactly alike."

"It is somewhat irregular, it is true. All-natural growths are more or less irregular—some more so than others. But, from the suggestions of these natural growths, we can draw regular shapes that are suitable for designs. I wish you, now, to take a small piece of paper and fold it in the middle. Near the crease, draw as accurately as you can the curve of half of your petal. Cut on this curve with your scissors, so that the folded paper petal falls out. Open your paper. What have you, Minnie?"

"I have a paper pattern, shaped very much like a petal of the dog-wood blossom."

"Why is not your pattern exactly the shape of the petal?"

"Because my pattern is exactly alike on both sides, and the petal is not."

"You may all see if you can trim your patterns, or cut another one, that is more nearly like the petal in shape than the first pattern you made. The patterns must all be alike on both sides. Perhaps those you cut at the first trial are too wide at the top or too narrow, or too pointed, or possibly the shape 0f the notch is not as it should be. Cut several patterns, if necessary, until you have a shape that is as nearly like the flower shape as possible, and is perfectly balanced."

"Our next step is to lay our paper petal in one of the divisions of our circle; place it between any two of the radii, not over a radius. Alice, do you think your pattern fills the space (a quarter-circle) as well as it should?" Remember that we are to repeat the form four times about a center; each unit should, in this case, use nearly all the space allowed for it."

"I think my pattern is too small."

"Yes, no doubt you will all wish to enlarge your units. I will draw a circle on the board, with the four radii like yours, and sketch, in one of the quarter sections, a shape that I think is large enough, and you may decide whether your patterns should be enlarged or not, in order to properly fill your spaces. You may trace and cut an enlarged pattern, correcting and changing it until it seems well adapted to your quarter-circle. Then trace around the pattern, moving it to each field, until four repeats are made. Join the outline of the petals somewhat as I have joined the units in the sketch on the board. When your rosette is complete, cut out the shape of the rosette, cutting on the lines that appear heavy in the blackboard sketch."

NOTE: For the teacher's suggestion in making this sketch, Fig. 1 is given below.

After having made a decorative form, the pupils will be much interested in applying it to some object that may be used. A pen-wiper suggests itself as particularly appropriate. In order to secure the right color combinations, the material would better be purchased expressly for this use. Three tones of brown, green, red, blue or violet may be used. Talk with the pupils about the kind of material best for wiping pens. Bring out the idea that the commonest articles of daily use may be thoughtfully planned and artistically finished.

Fig. 2 shows a pen-wiper made of three tones of brown flannel. The middle tone is used for the larger circle at the bottom; this is a circle that is 3½ inches in diameter. Several circles, 3 inches in diameter, are cut from the darkest tone; these are the "wipers." The decorative top is cut from the lightest tone, using the paper pattern prepared from the dog-wood blossom. The several circles are then arranged as shown in Fig. 2, fastened together with a cross-stitch, and finished with a small, flat button, of suitable color.

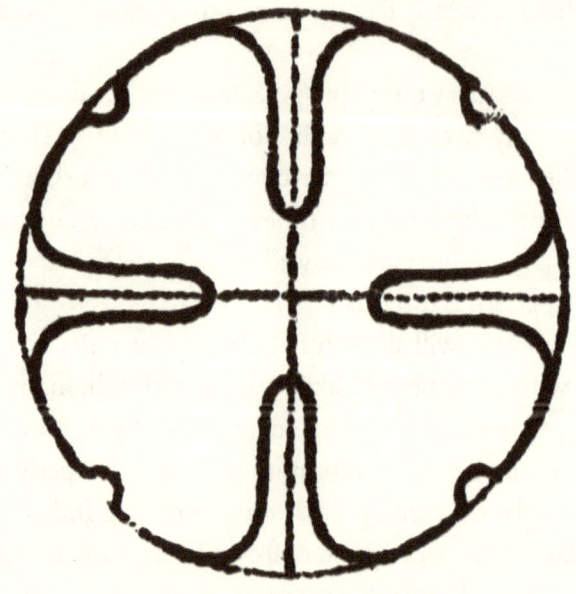

Fig. 1

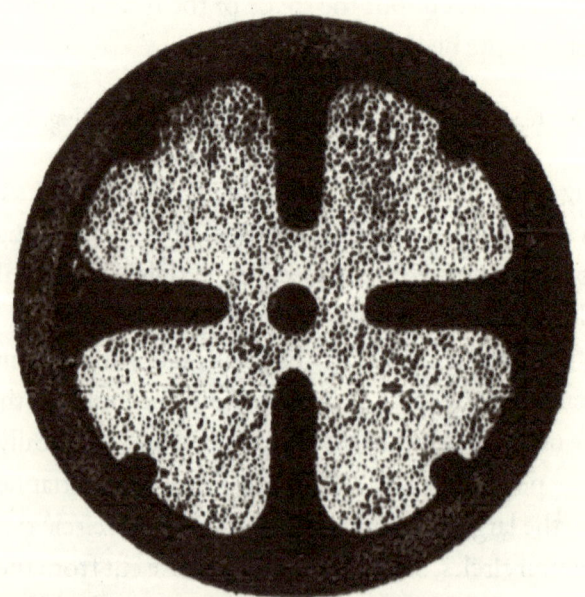

Fig. 2

SUGGESTIVE LESSON NO. 6.
Subject: Animal Drawing
(For Intermediate Grades)

In the primary grades, animals have doubtless been drawn or painted to some extent, but such work has probably appeared in connection with illustrative drawing, in which animals are sketched from memory. Or, if it has been possible for sketching to be done from animals brought to the school room, there has been, probably, very little analysis of forms or proportions. In the intermediate grades the methods of presentation are different in this as well as in other divisions of drawing. The pupils are now to study animals in the same spirit that they are led to study still life objects, flowers, or the landscape—as features of their environment, as parts of their life. For this reason, we cannot afford to neglect so universal an interest as animals in planning an educational course.

The common domestic animals should be studied from life. In every schoolroom, some pupil will be found who is willing to bring a pet dog, cat, rabbit, or pigeon to school. Or, a hen, rooster, duck, goose, or turkey may be borrowed or rented from a market, if these fowls are not procurable from the homes of the children. Of course, the animals must not be expected to "pose," or to keep a fixed position for any length of time. But their presence in the schoolroom will enable the children to study their proportions and their characteristics, even if their positions are constantly changing.

There are many interesting ways of beginning this work, with pupils who have not studied animals seriously before. As a preliminary exercise, the pupils may be asked to draw, in mass or outline, any animal that they can remember. Select ten or a dozen of these attempts, place them before the class and call upon the pupils to name them. After this experience, the pupils will probably realize the necessity of a closer observation of animals than they have before given.

Paper Cut Animals

Designs on Squared Paper

A Decorative Treatment of a Plant Form

Objects That Are Like a Sphere

Action Silhouettes

Let us suppose that a fox terrier has been brought to school for the lesson. If he is a well-trained dog, he may be induced to stand, sit or lie upon a table, in front of the school. The pupils are supplied with practice paper, charcoal or soft pencil, and the Drawing Book for the grade in which they are working.

"We have a distinguished visitor with us, today, who has consented to remain a short time, so that we may make some sketches of him, from life. As we do not wish to weary our guest or to impose too much upon his patience, we must work faster than usual and try to get just as many sketches as possible while he is here."

"Open your Drawing Books to a picture of a dog. Is our model like any one of the dogs you see, Philip?"

"He looks a little like the middle picture in the top row, but his head is a different shape."

"What is the difference?"

"The dog we are to study has a narrower head, and a longer and more slender nose."

"Do you see any other points of difference, Jessie?"

(The pupils give various points of difference and of similarity between the dog before them and the sketches before them.)

"Let us study the lines of our dog, as he stands before us." (The dog is supposed to have taken a position in which some of the pupils, at least, can see him in side view.) Of course, he will change his position frequently, but we can all see him, at different times. sufficiently well so that we can rapidly draw a few lines locating the back of the head, the end of the nose, the size and direction of his neck, the line of his back, the underline of his body, the length of his body, the height of his legs, and the mention of his tail. By the time you have done this, or before, he will probably have changed his position. But from any position he takes, we can study these general proportions. Much of our work must be done from memory, and having the dog before us gives us a chance to refresh our memory as often as is necessary.

Having the shape of our dog blocked in, we can now compare our quick sketch with our model. "What do you find to be the trouble with yours, Rachel?"

"I think the head is too large for the body."

What do you think of yours, Harold?"

"My sketch shows the body too thick."

"And yours, Frank?"

"The legs in my sketch are too short."

(The pupils make various criticisms on their own work, brought out by questions from the teacher.)

"Of course, these first sketches of yours show proportions, only. But if proportions are wrong, no amount of careful finish will make the drawing good. Study the model again, as he stands or moves about, and make such corrections as you can, in the proportions of the parts your first rough lines express.

"When you have corrected your errors, study your model again, this time for the location of ears, eyes, nostrils, etc. Correct the placing of these parts after careful observation and comparison of your sketch with the dog. You are now ready to draw carefully the shapes of the legs, body, head, and all of the parts. The dog will probably not stand still while you do this. You must seize your opportunity to study and draw the shape of any part that you can see. In finishing your drawing, try to give the outline a somewhat gray and accented quality, like the sketches in the book, to express the hairy or furry character of the dog's coat. Last of all, put in any characteristic markings or spots that the model shows."

After an exercise of this kind, the sketches of all the pupils should be displayed for class criticism.

SUGGESTIVE LESSON NO. 7.
SUBJECT: FIGURE DRAWING
(For Grammar Grades)

Before reaching the grammar grades, pupils are supposed to have made some progress in drawing from the figure. In the primary grades, drawing from the human figure, like animal drawing, is quite spontaneous in character, and is never subjected to rigid criticism or analysis. The children are, in those grades, chiefly interested in the various actions of the figure which they may desire to express in connection with their illustrations of stories or occupations. In the intermediate grades some analysis of proportions and parts has been made, and the pupils in grades seven and eight, if they have taken this work, know how to approach the subject.

They have already learned that the details which seem so important and so interesting to little children, such as the buttons on shoes or jackets, the decorative pattern of an apron or shirt-waist, ruffles, bows or other "trimmings," are really very unimportant indeed, compared with the leading lines of the figure, the proportionate length of head, waist, skirt or trousers, the length and positions of the arms, and the proportionate widths and depths of the figure. Perhaps they are so well grounded in essentials that they can slight the placing of the eyes, nose, mouth and ears, having found that a well-drawn figure of a pose is recognizable without the addition of features. They have found that in figure drawing, as well as in object or landscape drawing, attention to the big things leaves little to be done in regard to the drawing of the little things.

We will suppose that the lesson following is given to a seventh-grade class that has had the preliminary training suggested above.

"You will find on your desks a 6" x 9" sheet of light tinted paper a soft sketching pencil, and your regular Drawing Book. We are to draw today from a pose, and I wish you to select a girl who wears a dark skirt and a light waist. Who shall it be?"

"Lucy has a light shirt-waist, a dark skirt, and some dark bows on her hair."

"Very well, Lucy shall pose. Here is a large box for her to stand on. It will be easier for Lucy and will add interest to our sketch if we give her some occupation. What shall she do?"

"She might hold a book, as though she were reading."

"Yes, she may really read from this book, if she likes, or she might carry a basket or pail, a school-bag, or a package of books; or she might put her hat on and carry a suit-case or an umbrella, or a white hat-box. Lucy may decide what she would like to do."

"I think I would like to be reading."

"Very well. Before Lucy poses, let us open our Drawing Books and find similar figure sketches. Tell us about what you find, Howard."

"The sketches show two stages in the drawing of a figure. The left sketch shows what has been done first in putting in the leading lines."

"Yes; the proportions and parts of the figure have evidently been carefully studied before any masses have been laid in or definite drawing done. The head has been treated as a shape in itself, the waist has been blocked in, and the skirt handled in a similar way. The shape of the watering-pot, the arm, legs and feet have all been located. This sketch, you see, gives us the correct placing, the general shape, and the right size of all of the figure. Now Lucy may take her position on the box. Turn your side view to the class, Lucy."

Hold your book easily and naturally, as though you were reading a paragraph in class. "Henry, how tall shall we make our sketch?"

"I think it should be a little less than the height of our paper."

"Yes! on the paper you have today your sketch should be about seven inches high."

"About an inch from the top and near the middle of your paper make a light dash. This will locate the top of the head. An inch from the bottom, place another dash to locate the heel. All your measurements must fall between these two lines. With your vertical pencil held at arm's-length, measure from the top of Lucy's head to her waist line. Holding this measurement with the thumb, lower the pencil (still held at arm's-length) until the thumb hides the heel of the nearest foot. George, is the top of your pencil as high as the waist line?"

"No! it is quite a little below the waist line."

A First Sketch in the Study of a Pose

First and Second Steps in Figure and Action Drawings

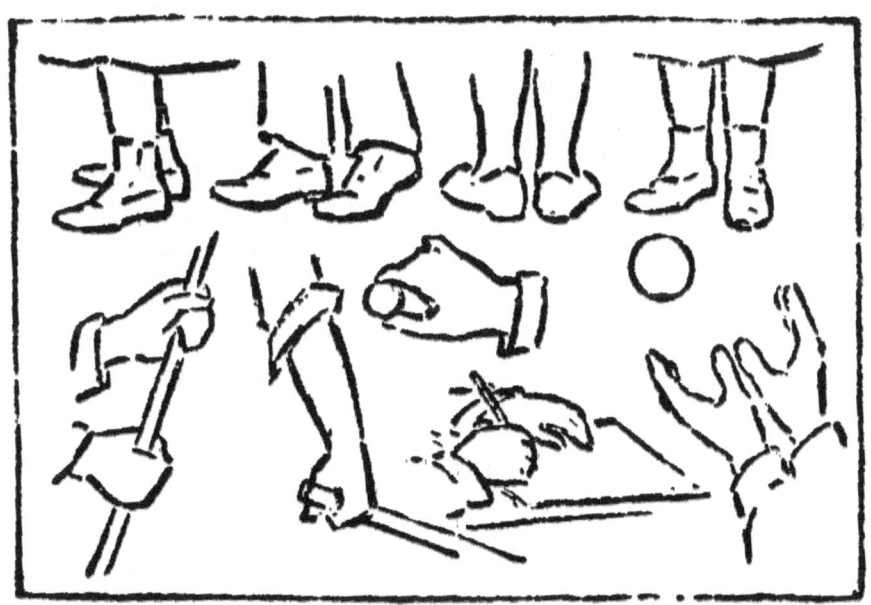

Showing Correct Drawings of Hands and Feet

"How do you find this measurement, Mary?"

"I find the same thing; the top of the pencil comes below the waist line."

"What does this show, Alice?"

"It shows that the distance from the top of Lucy's head to her waist is shorter than the distance from her waist to her heels."

"That is true. Look at the measurements on your pencil, and try to estimate this proportion. Then locate the waist in your sketch by placing a short dash where you think the waist should be. You now have three important points located—the top of the head, the waist and the heel. Measure again with your pencil, and find the height of the head as compared with the distance to the waist. Mark this on your sketch. Next, find by pencil measurement the length of the skirt. Locate this. We now have the important heights of the parts of our figure. We must next look for the various widths of our figure. Begin at the head. Measure again with your pencil the height of the head. Keep this measurement with your thumb, turn your pencil horizontally, and measure the width of the head at about the level of the nose. Indicate this proportion in your sketch with blocking-in lines, suggesting the shape of the head and face. Do the same with the shapes of the waist and skirt. Locate the height of the shoes and the width of the legs. Measure and locate the position and action of the arm and block in its shape, and also that of the book. Your drawing at this stage should have something of the appearance of the left sketch in the book. Lucy may rest while I pass about the room and glance at your blocked-in figures."

(Criticism of general proportions is very important at this point. The pupils should not be permitted to go further until their preliminary sketch is reasonably correct in proportion. It may take several lessons to bring this about.)

"Now we are ready for pencil rendering. Louis, look at the sketch in the Drawing Book, and tell me which are the darkest masses shown there."

"The ribbons, the collar, the belt and the stockings."

"Which masses are next in value, Martha?"

"The skirt and the shoes, I think."

"And which masses are a little lighter still, Alfred?"

"I think the masses of the hair and the watering-pot."

"Yes, I think so. And which are the lightest of all, Hilda?"

"The masses for the face, the hand, and the waist."

"Peter, how many values in all have been used in the sketch?"

"I think about four values."

"Let us see if we can express as much in our sketch and use only four values. Lucy, will you stand again, please? With long strokes that follow the direction of the hair (its arrangement and growth) lay on the value of the hair, trying to secure the value you desire at one stroke. We must express the value of *Lucy's* hair, remember, not the value of the girl's hair in the book. Next, decide on the value you need to express the dark ribbons. Lay this value on with forceful, vigorous strokes, obtaining the crisp, dark effect at once. Going over pencil strokes a second time always injures the drawing. Determine the value of the skirt. Observe the length of the pencil strokes used in laying in the mass for the skirt in the book, and try to get a similar handling in your drawing. Finish the other parts in the same way, after deciding on the right values. The waist, face, hands, and any other light values are to be expressed in outline, their values being shown by the value of the paper. Outlines for these parts should be gray and expressive, with occasional accents. Tomorrow we will have a class criticism of the sketches made today."

THEY MIGHT NOT NEED ME; YET THEY MIGHT
I'LL LET MY HEART BE JUST IN SIGHT;
A SMILE SO SMALL AS MINE MIGHT BE
PRECISELY THEIR NECESSITY.
EMILY DICKINSON

ABCDEH

WILLIAM
CAXTON
ENGLAND
CHAUCER
CANTER=
BURY TA=
BARD INN
FIRKINS
PJQVZ

Practical Alphabets with a Suggestive Spacing of a Quotation

Practical Alphabets and Numerals, Showing Suggestive Spacing of Letters

SUGGESTIVE LIST OF ART BOOKS AND ART MATERIALS

Art Books

Graphic Drawing Books, Nos. 1, 2, 3, 4, 5, 6, 7, 8 and High School.
Hand-painted Color Charts, Nos. 1 to 8
Outline Color Charts for Coloring, Nos. 1 to 8
Art Education for High Schools

Topic Books of Art Education

1. Pictorial Representation
2. Perspective Drawing
3. Figure and Animal Drawing
4. Mechanical and Constructive Drawing
5. Architectural Drawing
6. Design
7. Historic Ornament and Art History

How to Enjoy Pictures, by Mabel S. Emery
Illustrated Exercises in Design, by Elizabeth G. Branch
Pencil Sketching, by George Koch
Principles of Advertising Arrangement, by Frank A. Parsons
Principles of Art Education, by Hugo Munsterberg
Rugs in Their Native Land, by Eliza Dunn
With Pen and Ink, by James Hall
Twelve Great Paintings, by Henry Turner Bailey
Egypt: The Land of the Temple Builders, by Walter S. Perry
Booklet Making, by Henry Turner Bailey
Art of the Ages, by Marie R. Garesche
Geometric Problems, by C. W. Stoddard

Greek Myths and Their Art, by Charles E. Mann
How to Visit the Great Picture Galleries, by Esther Singleton
Manual Arts Portfolios in five parts
A Course in Mechanical Drawing, by Louis S. Roulllion
Nature's Aid to Design, by Bunce and Owen
Prang Neutral Scale of Values

ART MATERIALS AND WATER COLORS

Prang Water Colors

Water Color Box No. 1—four cakes
Water Color Box No. 2—three cakes
Water Color Box No. 3A—four cakes. No. 7 brush
Water Color Box No. 5—four whole pans semi-moist
Water Color Box No. 8—eight half pans semi-moist
High-School Water Color Box No. 16—sixteen half pans of semi-moist and two brushes
Water Color Cakes and Pans for "refills"
Moist Water Colors in Tubes—twenty-eight colors
Tempera Water Colors in Tubes—twenty colors

Tempera Board for Tempera Painting (send for sample)
Gold and Silver Paint
Mixing Tray
Stick Printing Dyes, 3 pans of color, 6 sticks
Weaving Papers in Book form—20 sheets, 20 colors
Water-Color Brushes—Nos. 6, 7, 8, to, and Double-end Brush (Nos. 4 and 7)
Double-Lipped Water Pan
French Charcoal

Prang Colored Crayons

Art Education Crayons, No. 1—8 small earth crayons, Tuck Box
Art Education Crayons, No. 2—8 large earth crayons, Hinged-cover Box
Crayonex, No. 3—8 wax crayons

Crayonex, No. 4—16 wax crayons
Crayonex, No. 5—4 large size crayons
Sepia Crayonex—8 wax crayons, Sepia Brown in Color
Hexagraph Crayons—8 wax crayons
Pastellex, No. 7
Artists' Pastel Crayons, 216 Colors
Colored Drawing and Construction Papers (send for Sample Booklet)
Drawing Papers—11 varieties (send for Sample Booklet)
Blotting Papers—8 tones (send for Sample Booklet)
Art Tablets—Nos. 1, 2, 3, 4, and 5
Assorted Package of Construction Papers (send for List of Tones)
Students' Envelope, Nos. 1 and 2 (send for List of Contents)
Mounting Board for Exhibitions, Nos. 1 and 2 (send for Samples)
Erasograph Paper

Prang Drawing Paper Assortments

Primary Assortment (send for List of Contents)
Grammar Assortment (send for List of Contents)

Prang School Drawing Portfolios

Paper Portfolio—two pockets
Cardboard Portfolio—with tapes
School Pencils,—Sketching, Hard, Medium, Soft-Medium, and Soft
Soap Eraser
Ink and Pencil Eraser

Prang India Ink

1 ounce, with penholder bottle
1 pint, bottle
1 quart, bottle
Round Pointed Scissors—4" blade
Sharp Pointed Scissors—4" blade

Temperine—⅛-ounce individual bottle; 2-ounce class bottle
Oil Dyes—eight colors
Permanent Mixture—4-ounce bottle

Prang Stixit Paste

4-ounce Collapsible Tube
4-ounce Large Mouthed Tin Can
½-pint Tin Can
1-pint Tin Can
1-quart Tin Can
1-gallon Tin Can

Prang Atomizer—Japanned, with hinge eyelet
Prang Stencil Brushes, No. 5—round—⅜-inch diameter
Prang Stencil Brushes, No. 7—round—½-inch diameter
Stencil and Woodblock Knife
Stencil Board cut—5 x 6, 10 x 12, and 20 x 24 inches
Ruco Printing Blocks—2½ x 2½ and 2½ x 5 inches
Arts and Crafts Tape, natural linen in spools of 100 yards
Stencillex—cotton fabric—by the yard, 36 inches wide or in packages of 25 pieces, cut 9 x 12
Hand-woven Russian Crash by the yard, 40 inches wide
Art Linen by the yard, 32 inches wide
Bookbinders' Crash the yard, 24 inches wide
India Net by the yard, 44 inches wide
India Floss in ¼-pound reels
Colored Raffia—eight colors and natural—¼-pound hanks

Prang Pottery Models

Set No. 1—6 models, different forms and colors
Set No. 2—8 models, different forms and colors
Set No. 3—10 models, different forms and colors
Bookplates—15 designs, put up 50 in a box (send for Circular)

Historic Ornament Plates—73 examples, 7 x 9 inches (send for Circular)
Wooden Models, Set No. 20—6 models, 1 x 2 inches
        Set No. 21—6 models, 1 x 2 inches
        Set No. 16—15 models, 2 x 4 inches

Prang Printing Outfit, large rubber type
Prang Color Prints, large colored pictures for school-room decoration
Hiawatha pictures, 8 pictures, in color
Diefenbach's "Wandbilder Friez" of silhouettes, 10 pictures, two sizes

www.ingramcontent.com/pod-product-compliance
Lightning Source LLC
Chambersburg PA
CBHW020431010526
44118CB00010B/519